Weather

By Alex Kimathi
Illustrated by John Robert Azuelo

Library For All Ltd.

Hot

Cold

Cloudy

Stormy

Windy

Drought

Rain

Short rain

Heavy rain

About the contributors

Library For All works with authors and illustrators from around the world to develop diverse, relevant, high-quality books. Visit libraryforall.org for the latest news on writers' workshop events, submission guidelines and other creative opportunities.

Did you enjoy this book?

We have hundreds more expertly curated original stories to choose from.

We work in partnership with authors, educators, cultural advisors, governments and NGOs to bring the joy of reading to people everywhere.

Did you know?

We create global impact in these fields by embracing the United Nations Sustainable Development Goals.

libraryforall.org

You're reading Learner

Learner – Beginner readers

Start your reading journey with short words, big ideas and plenty of pictures.

Level 1 – Rising readers

Raise your reading level with more words, simple sentences and exciting images.

Level 2 – Eager readers

Enjoy your reading time with familiar words, but complex sentences.

Level 3 – Progressing readers

Develop your reading skills with creative stories and some challenging vocabulary.

Level 4 – Fluent readers

Step up your reading skills with playful narratives, new words and fun facts.

Level 5 – Curious readers

Discover your world through science and stories.

Level 6 – Adventurous readers

Explore your world through science and stories.

Weather

First published 2024

Published by Library For All Ltd
Email: info@libraryforall.org
URL: libraryforall.org

This project was delivered with the support of Edmund Rice Foundation Australia.

Edmund Rice
FOUNDATION AUSTRALIA
Liberating Lives Through Education

Original illustrations by John Robert Azuelo

Weather
Kimathi, Alex
ISBN: 978-1-923339-78-1
SKU04511